All You Wanted
Chakras

Ravindra Kumar, Ph.D.
(Swami Atmananda)

New Dawn

NEW DAWN
An imprint of Sterling Publishers (P) Ltd.
A-59 Okhla Industrial Area, Phase-II, New Delhi-110020.
Tel: 6912677, 6910050, 6916165, 6916209
Fax: 91-11-6331241 E-mail: ghai@nde.vsnl.net.in
www.sterlingpublishers.com

All You Wanted to Know About - Chakras and Nadis
©2000, Sterling Publishers Private Limited
ISBN 81 207 2324 4
Reprint 2002

Published by Sterling Publishers Pvt. Ltd., New Delhi-110020.
Lasertypeset by Vikas Compographics, New Delhi-110020.
Printed at Shagun Composer, New Delhi-110029.

Contents

Preface

Kundalini energy is the basis of evolution and it works through the centres of energy, called *chakras*, and associated nerves, called *nadis*. Transformation of personality in a practitioner takes place gradually as the various chakras open up. It also depends on the nadis. Each one is important — the most important being *sushumna* through which the Kundalini is supposed to rise for self-realisation. It is the continuation of "Kundalini Yoga" on the practical side.

This book provides concise information on what one should know about *chakras* and *nadis*. The next book, titled 'Kundalini' is based on my personal experiences over the years of awakening, although a large number of publications have been consulted from time to time. An exhaustive theoretical study as well as practicals are possible at the Academy of Kundalini Yoga and Quantum Soul at any of its centres around the world. Things were made easy through computing and related facilities provided by Jytte

Kumar Larsen, to whom I am very grateful.

Swami Atmananda (Ravindra Kumar, Ph.D.)
Founder President
Academy of Kundalini Yoga and Quantum Soul
58-61 Vashisht Park, Pankha Road,
New Delhi-110046
Tel: 5047091, 5041368, 5034143, 5137567

Introduction

There are seven stations or *chakras* along the spinal column through which the Kundalini passes, on awakening. These stations are defined differently by different people according to their interest, training or perceptions. Thus, a doctor may call a chakra a bunch of nerves that forms the plexus, a clairvoyant may call it a vortex of energy moving in a circular path, a yogi or mystic may define them as points of varying consciousness, a tantric may define them as centres of paranormal powers, and so on. Each one of them is correct in his/her description since all these properties and some more are possessed by the chakras.

A chakra cannot be seen as a physical object since it belongs to the subtle realm. It can only be visualised through its properties, just as mind can be visualised through its thoughts, electricity can be visualised through the fan as it rotates, and so on. People engaged in *pranayama* activate energy, which can be seen through fluctuations in impulses recorded in chakra-machines which have been invented

,

recently. Similarly, the functioning of nadis can be measured and used for diagnosing disease tendencies before their manifestation through machines invented by, for example, Dr Hiroshi Motoyama of Japan.

Chakras are symbolised by lotuses, since a lotus corresponds to three different levels of spirituality. It is rooted in the mud - *ignorance*, endeavours through water to reach the top - *action*, and finally reaches out in the air to receive the light from the sun - *enlightenment*. This represents the quest of man from dusk to dawn. There are other things associated with the chakras, such as, colours, mantras, experiences, etc.

In layayoga one actually locates the trigger points of chakras and then concentrates on them. In kundalini yoga and kriya yoga one concentrates on reflections of actual trigger points on the front surface of the body. The sensation thus created on the surface passes to the chakra through the nerves and then to the brain in this order.

There are three psychic knots, called *granthis*, which may obstruct the path of the awakened kundalini. *Brahma granthi* lies around the root centre and it corresponds to inertia, attachment to objects of pleasure and selfishness. *Vishnu granthi* lies around the heart centre and it corresponds to action, ambition, passion, attachment to people and inner visions, *Rudra granthi* lies around the eyebrow centre and is related with attachment to paranormal powers (*siddhis*). For spiritual progress to be made, one has to take and pass tests at all the three levels.

It is through the awakening of the chakras that the practitioner gains awareness of and entry to the higher realms of existence. Practises of opening the chakras one after the other, is the practical side of kundalini yoga. Accordingly, it is advisable to study the theory of kundalini yoga before coming to the chakras and nadis, or the two should be studied in association. Although I had been a professor of mathematics for more than thirty years, having taught in about eight countries, I regularly practised yoga and meditation. Therefore, the transformations through chakras are described according to my own experiences with kundalini over the years. Nevertheless, the classical experiences of established yogis have been the guidelines.

Hierarchy of Chakras and the Need of Awakening

There are seven chakras below the root centre, *mooladhar* (mool = root, adhar = support): *patal, mahatal, rasatal, talatal, sutal, vital* and *atal*. These chakras exist in the animal body and their evolution takes place automatically, since the animals cannot do yoga or meditation. Humans have already transcended these chakras, which are topped by mooladhar - the foundation of evolution in humans. Then there are six more in the humans, that is,

13

altogether seven chakras - *mooladhar, swadhishthan, manipur, anahat, vishuddhi, ajna* and *sahasrar*. Just as mooladhar is the top chakra of animal life, even so, sahasrar is the top chakra of human life. Above mooladhar one lives as human, and above sahasrar one lives as divine. There are also gradations in divine living itself.

Along with outer experiences of life, the inner experiences come through meditation as different chakras open up along the nervous system of nadis in the psychic body. Kundalini sleeps in mooladhar and needs to be awakened through efforts, it is not automatic. On awakening, it should pass through the chakras smoothly till it reaches its destination - sahasrar, and the result in *nirvana*. However, if kundalini is blocked at a certain chakra, it begins to manifest paranormal powers related to that chakra. This is bad, since one may develop an ego of possessing powers and use them, which blocks further spiritual development. Kundalini may return to the base if it has not crossed the third chakra, manipur. If manipur is crossed, kundalini does not return to the base.

One may begin concentrating on the first chakra for a few weeks and then go on to the second, and so on. In many cases, a particular chakra is already awakened and on discovering this fact, one should concentrate on that chakra only for full development. Other chakras will then easily open in course of time. By the ascent of kundalini through various chakras, one endeavours to awaken all the related parts of the brain, so that the whole brain can be awakened. Sufferings in the world are related to the responses of the mind rather than the circumstances of life. Hence the awakening of kundalini, the nadis and chakras, directly effects our daily life. Outstanding people in the world - researchers, inventors, scientists, artists, builders, musicians, writers, statesmen, saints, etc., - are the awakened ones. One of the ten commandments says that one should "love one's neighbour unconditionally", but it does not happen. However, a person with awakened *anahat chakra* (heart centre) is invariably seen to love everyone unconditionally.

The difference between an awakened and an unawakened

person can be further understood through some famous examples. Apples used to fall from trees everyday, but no one took any notice of it. It was only Isaac Newton who noticed the falling apple and discovered the laws of gravitation. Take another example, Gautam Buddha and his brother Devdutt went to hunt in the jungle. Devdutt shot an arrow at a pigeon and killed it, and he was happy at his success in shooting. Devdutt felt no pain, but Buddha did. Buddha rushed to the pigeon and removed the arrow from its body. He felt the pain of the bird which gave rise to compassion — a proof of the sensitivity of the awakened one. Values of life change with the awakening.

The Nadis

The three nadis are - (i) *Ida*, (ii) *Pingla* and (iii) *Sushumna* - which create chakras (1) to (7) as shown in figure 1. The function of the chakras is to govern all aspects of our being and to supply energy to meet the basic needs. The seat of the kundalini is at the base of spine, between the first and second chakras, where it lies dormant in the form of a snake with three-and-a-half coils around the *swayambhu ling* and closing the opening of the ling with its mouth. Kundalini is

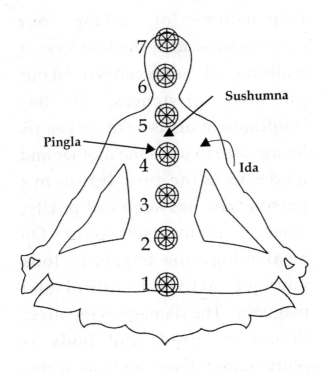

7

6

Sushumna

5

Pingla

4

Ida

3

2

1

Nadis and Chakras

responsible for taking our consciousness to the highest level of realisation. It has records of all our previous existences, it has intelligence of its own, gives its loving care to us as the mother and guides us as the guru. It rises in a person who has achieved purity, since it is in itself pure. On awakening, one begins to look younger, active, beautiful and magnetic. The damage is repaired, illness is cured, and body is rejuvenated. One can heal others too.

In the set of three nadis, Ida (moon channel) manifests at the left,

Pingla (sun channel) manifests at the right and the Sushumna constitutes the central channel. Ida and Sushumna start from the mooladhar chakra while Pingla starts from the swadhishthan. They all cross each other at the ajna chakra from where Ida moves to the right and Pingla moves to the left and three of them join again at the sahasrar.

Ida represents inertia (tamo-guna), past and subconscious. Its positive aspects are existence, emotions, joy, desire and auspiciousness. Its negative aspects are conditioning, superstition, lethargy, guilt, blind faith, self-pity, fear, day-dreaming, addictions, pornography, sexual perversions, and black magic.

Since emotion is born out of desire, the left side of the body represents the emotional side. If the left side is weak, one is prone to emotional extremism. The negative aspects of the nadi are manifested and the growing pressure on the brain can lead to a breakdown; in extreme cases one may become epileptic, lunatic, etc. A balance should be achieved through activity (*rajo-guna*) of the right channel. If the left side is strong, the positive aspects of the nadi are manifested and consequently, one expresses joy, buoyancy, happiness, etc.

Pingla represents activity (rajo-guna) and desire, future and supraconsciousness. Its positive aspects are physical and mental activities, creativity and self-respect. The negative aspects of Pingla are egotism, temper, tendency to dominate, cunningness, exploi-tation, vanity, shamelessness, fanaticism and asceticism.

With a strong right side the person is known to be egotistic,

25

selfish and aggressive. This may paralyse one's emotional side and the person may not be able to use logic and his inherent wisdom. A balance can be achieved by moving to the purity (*sattva-guna*) of the central channel, sushumna and in believing strongly, "I am not the doer."

Sushumna represents purity (sattva-guna), present and the unconscious. It has only positive aspects, such as, faith in religion, nourishment and revelation. It is the channel through which evolution takes place. When partly active, it provides awareness, virtue and righteousness. Kundalini, on awakening, first ascends through Sushumna upto the ajna chakra, and then descends through the Ida and Pingla in the molten form. The disparate factors of our being begin to integrate into a whole. It connects the mind to the soul (*atman*). Passing through the gate of ajna chakra one reaches sahasrar, where one finds the 'Kingdom of God'. Meditation makes the Sushumna strong. One lives in "eternal now", transcending time and space.

Arousal of kundalini through the Ida manifests its negative aspects. Arousal through Pingla manifests its negative aspects too; it is only arousal through Sushumna that leads one to the kingdom of God (*Sat-Chit-Ananda*).

The two nadis, Ida and Pingla create ripples through their respective powers and the points where these ripples meet, are called chakras. The chakras are vortices of energy, moving in clockwise direction. Each chakra corresponds to a plexus and to a certain number of petals expressing its qualities. Each petal in turn corresponds to a sub-plexus. Seen from above, the chakras would appear as overlapping circles.

Before the awakening of the kundalini, the chakras have a limited exhaustible energy, likened to a battery. After awakening, however, they are connected to the unlimited divine power plant through the *kundalini* and then their energy is inexhaustible. These chakras evolve and develop at various stages and they represent the milestones on the path of evolution. The methods that awaken chakras are called "Kundalini Yoga Practices."

The first and the lowest chakra in human body being the mooladhar, we begin our study of the chakras with it. However, yogis have laid greater importance on the ajna chakra, and according to them one should have all practises directed towards the awakening of this chakra. Ajna and mooladhar are related internally to each other and the awakening of one leads to a swift awakening of the other. If mooladhar is awakened first, it normally leads to some psychic problems which may be difficult to overcome. But if ajna is awakened first, all other chakras are easy to awaken and there are no psychic problems.

In fact, some yogis have awakened only ajna and the rest is seen to follow automatically. This is exactly what I have done in my life. All practices given in my books are directed towards the awakening of the ajna chakra, leaving the rest to nature. Nevertheless, in integral path of the yoga, we direct our attention to all the seven chakras from the lowest to the highest, but mainly concentrate on the ajna. One must, however, follow the direction of one's guru, if you have one.

Mooladhar Chakra

Mooladhar chakra (root centre) is situated slightly inside the perineum, and at the mid-point between the anus and scrotum in the males. It lies on the posterior side of the cervix in the females.

The vestigial gland called Brahma granthi lies at mooladhar which blocks the energy. With constant thinking of divine thoughts this knot begins to loosen its hold, and the moment it is opened, consciousness is liberated from the animal instinct and rises to psychic and spiritual experiences.

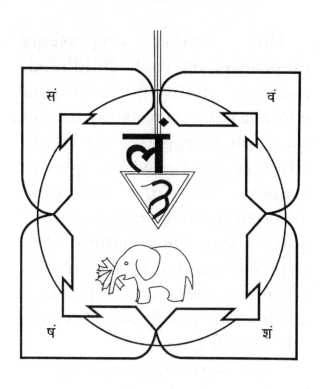

Mooladhar Chakra

This chakra represents innocence, eternal childhood, chastity, motherly love and wisdom. It is responsible for sex and excretion. Its negative aspects are adultery, perverted sex, pornography, lustful attention, materialism, no interest in spiritual quest, and constipation. The elephant God - Lord Ganesha, who is known as the remover of obstacles and the source of absolute wisdom, is its presiding deity.

After awakening, one achieves "victory over sex", and one learns to respect one's own chastity and that of the others. A child-like mind goes through the process of maturing and one is freed from sin. Sin in yogic terms means an intentional repetition of well-known mistakes, and so, it is in one's own power to achieve freedom from sin. With the eradication of selfishness, one always lives in the spirit of gladness.

Symbol
It is represented by a lotus flower with four petals of deep crimson colour. Letters *vam, sham, sham, sam* are written on each petal in golden colour. A golden yellow square represents the earth element and has an elephant with seven trunks representing the seven vital

minerals, called *sapta dhatu* in Sanskrit. The elephant being the largest and strongest of animals symbolises that great dormant power which rests in the mooladhar. A red inverted triangle rests on the back of the elephant symbolising creative energy or *shakti* — for productivity and multiplicity of things of all kinds. The Swayambhu ling in a smoky-grey colour is inscribed on the triangle, representing astral body. Around the ling, the kundalini, in lightening lustre, is coiled three-and-a-half times. The three coils represents three virtues (*gunas*) and the half represents transcendence. The letter *lam* rests on top of the triangle. Sense (*tanmatra*) associated with the mooladhar is "smell". On the awakening of this chakra psychic smells may be manifested, and the sense of smell becomes so acute that one cannot bear offensive odours. The chakra relates to the first of the mortal planes called *bhu lok*. It is the seat of the body of nourishment (*annamayakosh*) — absorption of food and excretion.

Relation to sex
Sexual act has a threefold purpose — procreation, pleasure, opening gateway to higher consciousness

depending on the level of interest. A yogi is supposed to have transcended the first two, and he/she concentrates only on opening the "window for samadhi", by generating an experience and sublimating it repeatedly. A female can get her mooladhar and swadhishthan awakened through the sexual act with a male yogi. However, a male has to get the awakening through one of the yogic practices.

Experiences

Awakening of mooladhar is associated with sensation of levitation (only a feeling, no actual floating of body), clairvoyance, heating sensation, creeping sensation (e.g., a small snake rising along spine), etc. Repressed emotions and passions are precipitated which may not be easy to control sometimes. If ajna is simultaneously awakened, troubles are almost nil, and breaking of animal bonds leads to expansion of awareness.

Practices for awakening
Trataka (gazing at a point)
Nosetip gazing is very helpful since sensory cortex representing mooladhar is connected with the

nose. After some practise, the two lines of nose will merge into one. Maintain the gaze on the tip, become aware of the breath and the accompanying sound, and be completely absorbed in the process. Gradually, increase the time from one to five minutes, according to your convenience. Gazing at the *OM* in red helps in opening both mooladhar and ajna simultaneously.

Location and concentration

Sit in *siddhasana*. Bring awareness to the whole body for some time, then direct it to the contact point between the heel and perineum. Take help through imagination of location described in the beginning.

Tribandh

Apply *moolbandh* (root lock), *uddiyanbandh* (navel lock) and *jalandharbandh* (chin lock) with *pranayama* (breath retention). The attention should be at the trigger point of mooladhar. The duration should be as long as one can comfortably do it.

It is advisable to practise the opening of ajna simultaneously for reasons explained earlier.

Swadhishthan Chakra

Swadhishthan chakra (pelvic centre) lies at the base of the spine. It can be felt as a small bony bulb just above the anus at the level of the tail bone or coccyx. Some say that it is suspended like a satellite on a chord from the manipur chakra above the genitals. In Sanskrit, *swa* means 'own' and *adhishthan* means 'abode', so that, *swadhisthan* means 'one's own abode'. It is related to the reproductive and urinary systems and corresponds to the prostatic

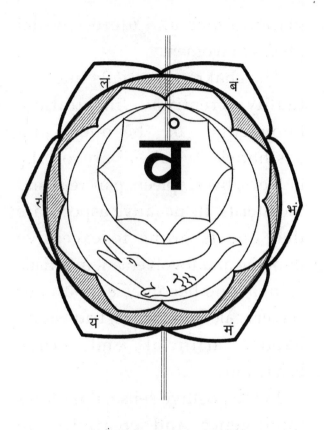

Swadhishthan Chakra

43

gland in men and utero-vaginal
plexus in women.

The chakra represents intellec-
tuality, creativity, inspiration,
knowledge of beyond, and
aesthetics. It takes care of the
kidneys, liver, spleen, pancreas and
the uterus. Its negative aspects are
that one is prone to excessive
thinking and involvement in artistic
things, one becomes egoistic, or
slavery, alcohol, drugs, bad eating
habits, artificial and crude
behaviour.

In the positive sense, it bestows
intelligence and creativity, in
conjunction with the Pingla nadi,

since its presiding deities are Lord Brahma and its power lies in Saraswati. Brahma is the creator and Saraswati is the goddess of music and arts in the Hindu mythology. Since Pingla draws its power from sushumna, an imbalance may be created which may result in diseases like diabetes and heart attacks.

A balance can be restored through non-materialism and non-egotism. Excessive thinking and attention can pressurise the liver. Interest in the knowledge of the dead, or black magic are wrong pursuits which can damage the chakra. One should aim at achieving the state of "thoughtless awareness" *nirvichar samadhi* and develop real humility. Increased awareness, ability of well-reasoned discourse, or writing of prose or verse are the gifts of the chakra. Freedom from enemies — greed, lust, anger, attachment and ego is achieved and one's mind dwells on the beauty of God. The poet may then touch the level of a prophet.

Symbol

The chakra is represented by a six-petalled lotus in vermilion or orange-red colour. Since it is the seat of ignorance, one can relate it to the black colour while undergoing experiences. Letters *bam, bham, mam, yam, ram* and *lam* are written, one on each petal, in the colour of lightening. A white crescent moon in the pericarp symbolises water element of the chakra. Inward turned petals signify storage of *karma,* and outward turned petals signify consciousness. The two yantras are separated by a crocodile, which represents the unconscious. Seed mantra *vam* in stainless white is seated on the crocodile. The sense (*tanmatra*) which is connected to the chakra is taste, the knowing organ (*gyanendriya*) is the tongue, and the

acting organs (*karmendriya*) are the
sex organs, kidneys and the urinary
system. The chakra is related to the
intermediate plane of awareness,
called *bhuvar lok*. Swadhishthan and
manipur are the seat of the body of
life (*pranamayakosh*).

Purgatory
The chakra being the storage of past
karmas, its awakening precipitates
negative *samskaras* to the surface,
which can be purgated once for all,
with the help of *pashupati* (pashu =
animal, pati = master) Lord Shiva.
According to the *Rig Veda*, it is the
universal womb (*hiranyagarbha*)

where everything exists in a potential state. Kundalini is seen to return to the mooladhar repeatedly after awakening initially because of the karmic block at swadhishthan. Many difficulties like lethargy, depression, indolence, sexual fantasies, passions, etc., may come in the way. A practitioner may encounter horrifying dragons or enticingly beautiful woman in their dreams and visions, testing their endurance. Only with the true understanding that the desires can never be satisfied, can one make the Kundalini pass through swadhish-than. Through determination and help from the guru, one can see through the body of beautiful alluring woman, and recognise her as the benevolent mother. When no kind of sexual desire disturbs the practitioner and when one is free of personal attractions, one can then think that the kundalini has gone past swadhishthan.

Practices for awakening
Location
Sitting in an easy pose, move a finger about an inch above the tail bone and press hard for about a minute. On removing the finger, a residual sensation will be felt.

Imagine a point about half an inch
deeper from the point of sensation;
this is the swadhishthan chakra.
Concentrate on the chakra for two to
three minutes with the repetition of
its name swadhisthan continually.
The counterpart of the chakra is in
the front of the body in the pelvic
bone at the end of the abdomen,
which should be pressed hard for
about a minute with the repetition
of the name swadhishthan. Now
contract the muscles of the anus
momen-tarily and release, again
contract and release, and so on. Feel
the waves so created, hitting the
chakra, with full awareness of the

point. This is called the *ashwini mudra* which should be continued for a few minutes.

Practice for males

Sit in a relaxed manner in a siddhasana with eyes closed. Pull the sexual organs upwards and contract the urinary system, similar to the situation when one has to control urination. Take care that the moolbandh or ashwini mudra are not performed simultaneously. Contraction and release should be done for ten seconds each. Concentrate on the pubis and repeat swadhishthan. This is called *vajroli mudra* which should be practised for a few minutes.

Practice for females

Sit in a relaxed manner in siddhasana with eyes closed. Place one of the heels inside the vaginal entrance and press against the walls, contract the vaginal muscles for ten seconds and then release, contract and release, repeating the name swadhishthan. This is called *sahajoli mudra* which should be practised for a few minutes.

Swadhishthan is internally connected with *bindu*, hence the two are affected simultaneously.

Manipur Chakra

Manipur chakra (navel centre) is situated at the level of the solar plexus on the inner wall of the spine, just behind the navel. In Sanskrit, *mani* means 'jewel' and *pur* means 'city', so the chakra means "city of jewels". Tibetans call it *mani padm* meaning "lotus of jewels". It represents righteousness, dharma (sustenance), desire of search, evolution, welfare, and wealth. This is the chakra of life force and takes care of the stomach, intestines,

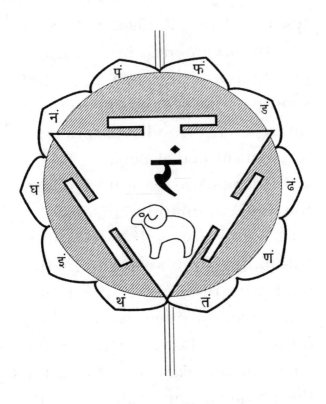

Manipur Chakra

spleen and liver. Its negative aspects are involvements in domestic problems, dominance over the spouse, either fasting or excessive interest in food, asceticism, materialism, and alcohol.

In the positive sense, it advocates the ten commandments as the guide-line for self-realisation. Kundalini first awakens in the manipur, piercing it from one extreme to the other. Its presiding deities are Lord Vishnu and Lakshmi, and so, care is taken for the physical and material well-being. Dharma and stomach seem to be related; whenever one revolts against dharma, one's stomach gets upset. However, after seeing the truth and beauty of the spirit on awakening, one does not care for worldly things and becomes a witness to the self. One learns to have faith in providence, gains strength to take responsibilities, and enjoys duties. Interest in alcohol and temptation for special dishes or fasting vanishes, and one's appetite is very easily satisfied.

One attains the power to create and destroy worlds through the power of speech. Presence of a saintly person is known to bring a sense of quietude and stillness into a group of tumultuous people. Manipur is at the boundary between the physical and spiritual worlds and its awakening normally brings visits to higher realms through astral bodies in dreams, trances and visions.

Symbol

It is represented by a ten-petalled lotus with bright yellow colour or with the colour of heavy rain clouds, according to Tibetans. Letters *dam, dham, nam, tam, than, dam, dham, nam, pam, pham* are inscribed on each petal in blue. An inverted fiery red triangle in the centre signifies the region of fire. Each side of the triangle has a T-shaped bhupura. At the bottom of the triangle is a ram with letter *ram* imprinted on it. Ram is the symbol of endurance and dynamism. The sense (*tanmatra*) is sight, as the organ of knowledge (*karmendriya*) are the eyes, and organ of action are feet. Manipur and swadhishthan are the seat of life (*pranmaya kosh*). Manipur corresponds to the last of the mortal planes called *swaha lok*, which is the heavenly plane.

Importance of manipur

It is said that mooladhar is the seat of kundalini, swadhishthan is its abode, and its awakening takes place in manipur. On awakening, the manipur kundalini does not recede. People practising yoga, living spiritual life, and looking for a guru have their kundalini in manipur and not in any lower centre. It is at the junction of two vital forces *prana* and *apana*.

Kundalini rises spirally as a hissing snake from mooladhar, while at manipur it awakens with a blast. Consciousness at manipur becomes spiritual and one gets a glimpse of higher planes or *loks*, which is not possible from the two lower chakras. It is for the first time on manipur that the personal problems, prejudices and complexes are dropped, after seeing the infinite beauty and perfection of the higher realms. A practitioner, with an awakened manipur is benevolent and compassionate, and he/she cannot misuse the psychic powers, which is likely with the darker aspect of the lower mind at the power chakras.

Practices for awakening
Tratak

One single and established method of hatha yoga which can awaken both manipur and ajna is *tratak* or gazing at a point without dropping the eye-lids. This is because manipur is directly connected with the eyes, and ajna and manipur are related in a way. I recommend gazing at OM in red from 15 minutes to an hour, slowly increasing the time. I advice this through my personal experiences. One can also practise by concentrating on a candle flame, then closing the eyes and concentrating on the inner image of the flame. This leads to inner tratak. Alternatively, one can follow the following mechanical procedure.

Location

Place a finger on the navel and a finger of the other hand directly behind it, on the spine. Press firmly with the finger on the back for about a minute and then remove the finger. Feel the residual pressure go deeper from that point, and concentrate there. This is manipur. The navel itself is the area in the front (*kshetram*). Concentrate on the manipur for a few minutes with the repetition of the word manipur.

Agnisar Kriya

Sit in a comfortable position. Take slow and deep breaths and watch the expansion and contraction of the navel. Feel the waves thus created, hitting the manipur, and feel that you are breathing through the navel. Keep repeating 'manipur' mentally. This is pre-kriya purification.

Sit in vajrasana. Join your feet but keep the knees separate. Place both the hands on the knees. Exhale completely and apply the jalandhar bandh. Now expand and contract the abdomen rapidly; you may do it 25 to 30 times in a holding, with gradual practise. Release jalandhar bandh, inhale and relax. Repeat the process four to eight times, slowly increasing the number. People with peptic ulcer and heart disease should avoid this kriya.

Tribandh
Exhale and apply moolbandh, uddiyan bandh and jalandhar bandh simultaneously, retaining it as long as possible. Keep repeating 'manipur'. Repeat process five to ten times.

Meeting of apana and prana

Sit in siddhasana, relax and observe the breathing process. Slowly one becomes aware of one life force (*apana*) travelling from the mooladhar to manipur, and the other (*prana*) travelling from above to manipur. At the feeling of the meeting of two forces at navel, retain your breath with the moolbandh and concentrate on the navel. Repeat the process few times depending on your convenience.

Anahat Chakra

Anahat Chakra (heart centre) lies on the inner wall of the spine just behind the centre of the chest, not the centre of heart. It is related to the cardiac plexus and is connected directly to that part of the brain which gives rise to creativity and fine arts in all possible ways. Anahat means unstruck. With the awakening of this chakra, one can hear, with the inner ear the cosmic sound - *AUM* or *WORD*, which is created without the striking of two

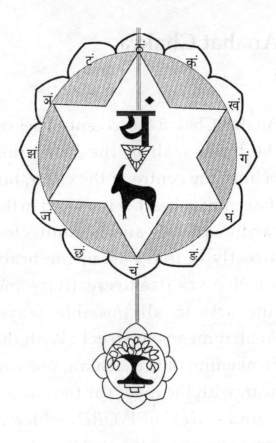

Anahat Chakra

objects; it is heard when all the internal noises of the mind have been stopped through sustained practise. The chakra represents existence, love, truth and truth-attention-joy (sat-chit-anand) after awakening.

Its negative aspects are extreme physical and mental activities, bad relations especially with the mother, drugs, no faith in God, and anti-God activities. Its presiding deities are Lord Shiva and Parvati or the *Atma* (spirit). On awakening, one loses identification with the body, mind and feelings, and one really becomes the spirit or atma because of an open and clean heart. Forgiveness and the all-pervading attention and care of Jagadamba, the mother of the universe are received. One develops reverence for one's physical mother, who has a place on the left of the heart and one's father, who has a place at the right of the heart. One realises that we actually choose our parents.

Pure love is detached and it works unconditionally, flowing like a river. Elimination of self-will and removal of self-protecting screen enables one to put oneself in another's shoes and to understand the person. Psychic powers here include hearing of sounds (buzzing of bees, flute, etc.) from the higher realms; becoming an inspired writer, poet, artist, etc.; attaining perfect health and the power of healing others; living peacefully under all circumstances, etc.

Symbol

It is represented by a twelve-petalled lotus in shining crimson colour according to the texts, but some saints, such as Swami Satyanand Saraswati, have experienced it in blue colour. Letters

kam, kham, gam, gham, anga, cham,
chham, jam, jham, nyam, tam and *tham*
are inscribed one on every petal in
vermilion colour. Its hexagonal
shape, represents the air element
(*vayu tattva*) and is made of two
interlaced triangles — the upright
one represents consciousness or
Shiva, and the inverted one
represent creativity or Shakti. Seed
mantra *yam* in grey in scribed on
black antelope represents alertness
and quickness. There is an eternal
flame (*akhanda jyoti*) or *ban ling* in
gold according to some, in the
centre, representing the soul

(*jivatma*). A subsidiary red lotus below contains the wish fulfillment tree (*kalptaru*). One can visualise the kalptaru or a blue lotus in the still lake inside the hexagon. Its sense (*tanmatra*) is touch, the sense organ (*gyanendriya*) is skin and the action organ (*karmendriya*) are the hands. Its vayu is *prana* and it belongs to *maha lok*, which is the first of the immortal planes. The chakra represents the body of mind and emotions (*manomayakosh*).

Second of the psychic knots or *Vishnu granthi* lies here. Before unification it represents the bondage to emotions and feelings, afterwards, one takes decisions based on spiritual quest rather than emotional attachments. A yogi with the awakened anahat is wise, doer of noble deeds, has senses under control and is adored by women.

Importance of Anahat

Below manipur, one is completely under the control of *prarabdha karma* and one's life is destined. At manipur, one gets some control over one's destiny, but one is still under prarabdha. At anahat, one can go totally beyond the dictates of destiny since consciousness has accelerated to the speed of free-will. Although gravity exists, one has attained the power of throwing things beyond gravity. One is now really a yogi, and standing under the wish fulfilment tree (kalptaru) whatever thoughts one has, positive or negative, they come true. One has to be alert like an antelope to guard against negative thinking.

However, the shastras have warned us. If one imagines being successful, one is successful; if one thinks of being doomed, one gets doomed. Avoid company of those who depend on fate. One should be always optimistic, every situation is good, and one should be always at peace, whatever the circumstances. There is a marked change in the level of thoughts on the awakening of this chakra, and it influences daily life events. Beware, if one falls from anahat, it is almost impossible to come back. It is unselfishness, unconditional love (there is no bargaining), and spiritual compassion that will make one move to the next - *Vishuddhi Chakra*. Bhakti yoga is one of the surest means of awakening the anahat.

Practices for Awakening

Location

Place a finger on the centre of the chest. This is the area (*kshetram*) of the chakra. Place the other finger just behind the first at the back of the spine. This is the anahat. Press the area with both the fingers firmly for about a minute and then remove. Concentrate on the residual sensation and keep repeating 'anahat'. Practise the whole exercise for a few minutes.

Bhramari Meditation

Before starting to meditate, it is better to purify oneself by observing your breathing while sitting comfortably. On expansion of the chest you can feel that you are breathing through the centre of the chest and passing it on to the chakra at the back. On contracting the chest feel the reverse, that the breath is flowing from the chakra at the spine, passing to the centre of the chest, and going out of the body. Keep repeating 'anahat'. Do this for a few minutes.

Now breathe in slowly and deeply, keeping the teeth slightly apart and your mouth closed, so that the vibrations can be experienced. While exhaling, produce a humming sound continuously till you exhale completely, and then stop humming. The eyes should be closed and the ears plugged with two fingers. One should practise this for five to ten minutes without straining oneself. The purpose is to feel the reverberation of the sound inside the head and concentrate on it.

Ajapa jap

Sit in siddhasana and be aware of the natural breathing as you inhale and exhale. There should be no effort to force the natural breathing. Now concentrate on the sound *so* while inhaling, and on the sound *ham* while exhaling. Become one with the mantra *so-ham* of the breath. After a while, try to be aware of the psychic sound *so* from navel to throat, and *ham* from throat to navel. Practise this way for about 15 minutes in the morning or in the night before going to bed. In about a month's time you will achieve automation. This is a very powerful way of awakening anahat.

Vishuddhi Chakra

Vishuddhi Chakra (throat centre) is located at the juncture of the spine and the medulla oblongata, in the cervical plexus directly behind the throat pit, taking care of the physical parts such as arms, face, throat, mouth and teeth, and suggest a protection from cold, smoking habits and negligence of dental care.

It represents collective conscious-ness, divine attitude, androgynous personality (balance of masculinity and femininity, acceptance of

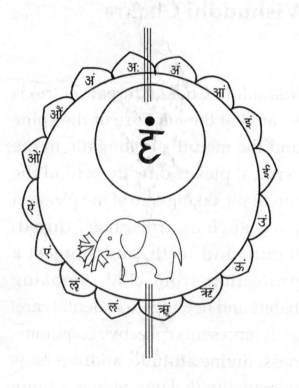

Vishuddhi Chakra

82

unpleasant and pleasant happenings equally), and playful witness. Its presiding deity is Lord Krishna with Radha for the centre of the chakra. Lord Krishna is the eternal witness, watching the cosmic drama with complete detachment. The deity of the left side of the chakra is Lord Krishna's sister Vishnumaya, representing brother-sister relationship on the positive side, and mortality, guilt, sarcastic attitude and foul tongue on the negative side. The deity of the right side of the chakra is Bal Krishna (Lord Krishna as child) representing witnessing of the self on positive side and smoking,. bronchial problems and cold, swearing, and chanting on the negative side.

Awakening of the chakra provides victory over the negative aspects of the left, right and central chakras and realisation of all the positive aspects. *Shuddhi* means purification, and the chakra can thus be called "centre of purification". Awakening promises freedom from 'worldly desires'. The energy hitherto used for achieving worldly goals, is now free and redirected upwards to open the gateway to liberation. Eternal knowledge from mooladhar and wealth of knowledge from manipur are combined as the union of subjective and objective, at the Vishuddhi, leading to the true meaning of yoga which is union. A shift from the intellectual to a deeper level gives peace of mind and an understanding of the past with clarity. It helps in seeing the present and anticipating the future. Increased awareness and greater discrim-ination clearly tells one about what should be done and what should be avoided. One becomes merciful to all, knowing that one is a product of one's circumstances and victim of one's own ignorance.

Symbol
It is represented by a lotus with sixteen petals, corresponding to the sixteen nadis, in dark grey colour according to tantra, and in purple colour according to Swami Satyananda Saraswati. Letters *am, aam, im, eem, um, oom, rim, reem, lrim, lreem, em, aim, om, aum, am, ah* are inscribed one on each petal. A white circle and an elephant within it, in

the pericarp represents etheric region (*akash*), opening the gateway to liberation for the purified and controlled one. The practitioner may visualise oneself sitting on the back of the elephant and being transported from the lower to higher consciousness. Vibration of etheric element is *ham* which is shown as the seed mantra in the circle. Its vayu is *udana* which sustains and lifts upwards. The sense (*tanmatra*) is hearing, organ of knowledge (*Gyanendriya*) is ears, and organ of action (*karmendriya*) is vocal chords. It belongs to the fifth plane called *janah* or *jnan lok*. Vishuddhi and ajna correspond to the psychic body (*vigyanmayakosh*).

Mooladhar and vishuddhi produce keynote sounds in *nada yoga*, and the chakras can be easily awakened through devotional singing (bhajan and kirtan).

Importance of Vishuddhi

Vishuddhi chakra is internally connected to bindu, an additional chakra between the sixth and seventh centres. A divine fluid or nectar (*amrit*) or the *somras* of the *Vedas* is generated at bindu, which rejuvenates the body and is the secret of the youth of yogis. Such a fluid is referred to in other faiths too. For example, the sweet wine of Sufi poets brings instant intoxication. Ritualistic wine in Christianity, which is consecrated and sacramentally imbedded, perhaps symbolises the same idea.

Before awakening of Vishuddhi this fluid goes waste, but after awakening it works as a nectar and spreads throughout the whole body. Degeneration and ageing process is arrested. Another potential of vishuddhi is the ability to understand the thoughts of others, as hinted earlier. This is due to the simultaneous awakening of another minor centre close by. Furthermore, with the awakening of tortoise nerve (*kurma nadi*) one attains the ability to live without food and drink.

Practices for Awakening
Khechari Mudra
Sit comfortably, close the mouth and roll the tongue backward as far as possible, press the rolled up tongue against the upper palate. Tip of the tongue will stimulate many vital areas upto and into the nasopharynx. Breathing should be normal. If one feels uncomfortable

then relax and repeat. Do it for few minutes. Now contract the glottis in the throat and continue breathing with the feeling that you are breathing through the throat. Soon you will begin snoring. Breathing should be slow and long. This is known as *ujjayi pranayama*. Continue for a few minutes, increasing the time everyday.

Note: It is advisable to practise jalandharbandh five to seven times before beginning the practice of khechari mudra.

Location and Purification
Put a finger on the glottis and the other finger on the spine just behind

the first finger. This is vishuddhi chakra. Press the fingers for about a minute and release. Concentrate on the residual sensation and mentally keep repeating 'vishuddhi'. After few repetitions apply khechari mudra and practise ujjayi pranayama. Gradually begin to feel that you are inhaling through the glottis (vishuddhi area or kshetram) and the breath is hitting the chakra at the spine. While exhaling, feel that the breath is returning from the chakra and escaping through the glottis. Continue this exercise for a few minutes.

Vipareet Karani Asana

Hold the body in *sarvangasana* with the difference that the trunk should make an angle of 45 degrees to the ground. Remain in the asana for ten minutes, then gradually increase the time. It is a strong "kundalini yoga" method for awakening the vishuddhi. It should be followed by *shavasana* (death pose) for a few minutes to counter the effect brought on by this asana and to bring normalcy.

Ajna Chakra

Ajna chakra (eyebrow centre) is the most important of the psychic centres. It is also called, "centre of command", "the eye of Shiva", the "guru chakra", and more popularly the "third eye". Astrologically, it is associated with Jupiter or Brihaspati. It is the centre where the three nerves-Ida, Pingla and Sushumna meet. Physically, this is signified by the meeting of the three rivers-Ganga, Jamuna and Saraswati at Prayag in the present

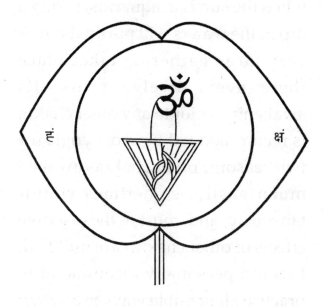

Ajna Chakra

day Allahabad in India. People believe that every twelve years when the sun is in aquarius, taking a dip in the waters will purify them. A very large gathering takes place there every twelve years. Its awakening prior to any other chakra is recommended by most yogis for two reasons: other chakras awaken much easily, sometimes simultaneously; and, most of the negative effects of other chakras are nullified. I would personally recommend to practise all possible ways to awaken ajna only. Other things will just follow.

Ajna chakra is located at the top of the spinal cord, at the medulla oblongata, and is connected to the pineal gland. Purification of the pineal gland guarantees the proper functioning of the pituitary and other glands and thus the chakra takes care of the whole body.

The presiding deity of the central chakra is Lord Jesus Christ representing forgiveness and resurrection, that of the left chakra is Lord Mahavira representing subconscious (superego). The deity of the right chakra is Lord Buddha representing *ahankar* (ego). The positive aspects of the centre are sight, hearing and thought and the negative aspects are bad association and wandering eyes. The positive aspects of the left are memories and conditioning from past, and the negative aspects are addictions and self-indulgence. The positive aspect of the right is egoism and the negative aspects are worries, harmful attitude towards others, and incorrect notions of God.

With the arrival of kundalini at this chakra, thoughtless awareness brings blissful silence which is the heart of creation; one is in direct communication with the creator and commands are received here. Yogis undergo an experience of death and ego is fragmented into millions of pieces. One enters the state of *shoonyata* (void) or absolute nothingness. This is one's second birth from mother kundalini with the blessings of Paramshiva. According to the message of Lord Jesus, one is resurrected and born again into a new awareness of the self. Karma is the result of past actions of ego, and oneness with the spirit takes one beyond ego and karma; vestiges of imperfection are purified and the karmas are burned away. God's compassion is expressed through our forgiveness, and the person forgiven may not be affected but our chains are broken.

One is now androgynous, *ardhanareeshwara* - half male, half female - having a perfect balance of intellect and intuition. One knows more than three or four dimensions, which cannot be described, it can only be experienced. One begins to feel grateful to even those who have been one's critics and made one's life miserable. However, temptations continue even in the life of saints and yogis, but they are more subtle now. The guru can make a mistake too, but a purpose may not be there.

Ajna gives the power of awareness and discrimination, but it should be crowned with compassion. Successful arrival at ajna is indicated by the realisation of its deity Paramshiva, according to traditional terminology, who shines like a chain of lightening flashes during meditation on ajna chakra.

Symbol
It is represented by a two-petalled lotus in pale-light-grey colour

according to scriptures, some say it is silvery white, yet some think it is intangible.

The left petal corresponds to the Ida or moon, and the right one corresponds to Pingla or sun. Letters *ham* and *ksham* appear on the two leaves in silvery white colour, which are the seed mantras of Shiva and Shakti. Circle represents void (*shoonyata*), and the inverted triangle in the circle represents shakti (*creativity and manifestation*). A black Shivalingam is placed on the triangle which represents "astral body", and not phallus as wrongly understood by some. The lingam appears in three colours: smoky at mooladhar, called *dhumra lingam*, representing instinctive consciousness; black in ajna, called *itarakhya lingam*, representing knowledge of self; and luminous in sahasrar, called *jyotir lingam*, representing illumination. So, according to the evolving consciousness in the practitioner, the colour changes from smoky to black to luminous. The seed mantra of ajna is OM that appears on top of the triangle, and the *raif* on top of it represents sound consciousness.

Its sense (*tanmatra*), sense organ (*gyanendriya*) and action organ (*karmendriya*) are all represented by the "mind" - since it perceives knowledge and acts upon it too. It belongs to the sixth plane called *tapa lok,* where purification and burning of karma takes place. Ajna and vishuddhi are related to the body of psychic development (*vigyanm-ayakosh*). As one meditates on the awakened ajna one sees a flaming lamp like the rising morning sun. Unity with Brahma and paranormal powers (siddhis) are achieved, according to the make up of the practitioner.

Importance of Ajna

Representing higher level of awareness, ajna is the chakra of the mind. Dreams, perceptions of daily happenings in life, and speculation of future, are all activities of mind. With an awakened ajna, one perceives intuitively without the use of normal senses, through the sixth sense. Having achieved purified intellect (*ritambhara buddhi*) one gets rid of attachment, fickleness of mind, ignorance, and lack of discrimination. Will-power (*sankalp shakti*) becomes so strong that one realizes fruits of mental resolve immediately. One becomes a detached witness to all happenings, meanings of symbols flash in the mind intuitively, and attachment to siddhis are transcended, which opens the third knot called *rudra granthi,* and the way to sahasrar is cleared. All dualities such as victory and defeat are transcended, one awakens from the "dream of life", just as one awakens everyday looking at the dream as a bygone thing, and most importantly, the law of cause and effect is understood — you are no more sorrowful and depressed about specific happenings in life. Nothing disturbs you, and you participate in all affairs of life fully and live as a detached witness. You flow with the fast current of life with a sense of surrender.

Practices for Awakening

Through the process of *jalneti* (circulation of water) one should clear the nasal passages. It also cures disorders of the ears, nose and throat and relieves one of cold and sinus effects. This facilitates clear concentration on ajna. In fact, concentration on ajna is difficult, and one is recommended to concentrate at the point between the eyebrows, called *bhrumadhya*. One can also use some cooling ointment or balm or *chandan* to feel the pressure of concentration there. Concentration eventually stimulates the pineal gland which results in internal experiences and visions.

Anulom Vilom Pranayam (incoming and outgoing breath)

Sit in a comfortable posture, with your spine straight and relaxed. Be aware of the process of inhaling from the tip of the nose, through the nasal passages, up to the bhrumadhya. Similarly while exhaling, be fully aware of breathing backwardly from bhrumadhya to the tip of the nose. After some time, complete a round by inhaling consciously through the left nostril to bhrumadhya and exhaling through the right, then by inhaling through the right nostril and exhaling through the left. Be conscious of the triangle with the apex at bhrumadhya and the base at the level of the upper lip, the two sides of the triangle being nasal passages. Practice 100 rounds like this. Remember:

- Breathe normally with both the nostrils after every four rounds.
- Awareness must be maintained.
- Count of 100, and not less, must be completed.

The practice will stimulate the unconscious in ajna, and one may be exposed to the impressions stored therein. One may even go into trance. This is a strong method of awakening ajna.

Trataka (gazing at one point)
This is the most powerful and useful method that gives good results. Concentrate on a central point of OM in red kept at the eye level at a

comfortable distance. Light on OM should be just enough to see it. There should be total concentration to the extent that one forgets the rest of the body and surroundings. One should concentrate without blinking, even if the eyes begin to water. When it becomes quite uncomfortable, close the eyes and relax. One can replace OM by the image of God or guru or any other object. But remember that OM is the gateway to God. One may concentrate internally on a point of light or star or deity, etc. However, concentration should be maintained at one selected point. The duration can vary from 15 minutes to one hour. The following benefits are accrued by the practice:

- Physical: Some weaknesses and defects of the eyes are corrected.
- Mental: Anxiety of mind is relieved, insomnia is cured and nervous stability is achieved.
- Spiritual: The mind stops wandering and sustained concentration awakens the ajna eventually, leading to various experiences.

Shambhavi Mudra

Sit in a comfortable posture with your spine straight, look at a point as high as possible and bring the gaze to bhrumadhya. Keep repeating OM (every two seconds) in a soft and clear voice and maintain the awareness of the sound of the mantra in bhrumadhya. Practise for five minutes.

Now close the eyes, continue to concentrate on bhrumadhya, chanting OM in a long and continuous manner. Awareness of the sound emerging from bhrumadhya should be maintained. Practise for five minutes. Now continue to chant OM in a long

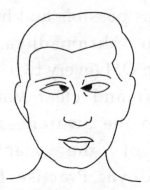

Shambhavi Mudra

manner and be aware of the sound emanating from bhrumadhya which reverberates through the whole body. Practise for five minutes. Take care that the eye muscles are not strained. The period for practise can be gradually increased with time.

Bindu Chakra

Bindu chakra (point/drop centre) is situated at the back of the head at a point where Hindus tie a tuft of hair, called *shikha* in Sanskrit. This tuft is pulled and tightened so that the person can concentrate on this sensation while repeating the mantra and awaken the bindu.

The real purpose of the tuft is now forgotten but the custom continues. Bindu and vishuddhi are internally connected through nerves, accordingly when

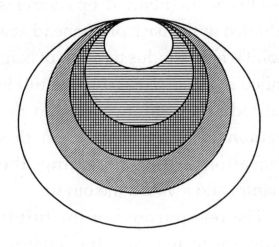

Bindu Visarga

vishuddhi awakens bindu also awakens. Nectar flows from bindu and drops in vishuddhi, from where it spreads into the whole body, resulting in rejuvenation as the ageing process is arrested. There is a small depression or pit in the upper cortex of the brain containing a minute secretion. There exists a small elevated point like an island in the lake, and this is bindu. There have been cases where yogis gradually cut the frenulum of the under surface of the tongue, which is thus elongated and blocks the passage at nasopharynx by insertion. Bindu is stimulated, nectar flows and the person can now hibernate for several days. Such a person can live without food and breathing for a long time. However, such extreme cases are rare.

Symbol

It is represented by a crescent moon on a moonlit night. Crescent moon represents the various phases of moon corresponding to mental and emotional fluctuations in humans. Just as the moon is gradually revealed, sahasrar (crown centre) is gradually unveiled through persistent yogic practices. Night sky in the background represents the infinite nature of sahasrar beyond bindu. Only when individuality is lost, is sahasrar revealed. It relates to the seventh and the highest plane of truth, called *satya lok*, and corresponds to the causal body (*anandmaya kosh*). On awakening of the bindu, one hears the cosmic sound of OM and realises the source of all creation through bindu.

Importance of Bindu

Bindu is the gateway to infinite void (*shoonyata*), where zero and infinity, nothingness and fullness exist simultaneously. Spiritual energy first enters through the bindu before creating multiple individual forms of the universe. Inherent potential of consciousness accumulates at bindu and creates myriads of objects. Every object of the universe has a bindu, which lies in the womb of creation (*hiranyagarbha*). The creative spiritual force enters the body through bindu and returns to the source through bindu which is the trap-door of cosmos. It is through bindu that the consciousness enters sahasrar, after perfection through the evolutionary yoga. According to the "big bang" theory, an infinitely dense point exploded and created the universe. According to *the Yogachudamani Upanishad* (verse 60), "The bindu is of two types - white and red. The white represents sperm (*shukla*) and the red represents menses (*maharaj*)". The white one lies in bindu symbolising Shiva and the red one lies in mooladhar symbolising Shakti. Any system of yoga is the means to unite these two opposites, that is, male principle (*purusha* or consciousness) and female principle (*prakriti* or manifestation). It is through this union that the kundalini ascends and the practitioner attains divinity. Verse 64 of the same *Upanishad* says, "He who realises the essential oneness of the two bindus, when the red bindu merges with the white bindu, alone knows yoga."

Practices for Awakening
Exact location of bindu is not straight forward and easy to find like other chakras. When the inner sound has been generated through yoga practices, one can trace the source of sound back to bindu. To this end, any of the following practices can be adopted, each

leading to the same result: *bhramari pranayama, moorchha pranayama, vajroli mudra and yoni mudra.* Bindu and swadhishthan are related in the sense that the division of energy into male and female principle is physically represented by the sexual function of swadhishthan. Material union of sperm and menses is the prototype of the union of soul and supersoul.

Moorchha Pranayama

Sitting in siddhasana, perform the khechari mudra. Perform ujjayi pranayama, lean the head backwards, and perform shambhavi mudra. Inhaling slow and deep, see that the head is partially backward at the end of inhalation. Retain the breath as long as possible with attention on bindu while observing the shambhavi mudra. At the end of exhalation, the face will bend forward with eyes closed. Release khechari mudra, relax the body, and breathe normally. Observe that the mind is becoming light and calm. Begin the second round after some rest and do ten or more rounds till you feel weak. One should stop here otherwise this can lead to unconsciousness. Withdrawal of senses (*pratyahar*) is best achieved this way.

Vajroli with Bindu

Immediately after murchha one should come to vajroli. Observe vajroli mudra with repetition of swadhishthan mentally. Now take the awareness from swadhishthan to bindu through sushumna and feel that sexual energy is uniting with its source at bindu. Keep repeating mentally 'bindu'. Return to swadhishthan and release vajroli. Repeat the process and complete about 25 rounds.

Bhramari and Bindu

Observe the bhramari pranayama for a while, keeping your ears closed, concentrate on listening to an inner sound. In the beginning, you may not find one but gradually you will discover one, which will become louder and louder. Be completely aware of the sound. After some practise another faint sound will be heard. Concentrate on this new and faint sound which will increase one's perception. Repeat the process and you may discover another faint sound, which should be concentrated upon. Go on like this and increase the time, gradually. Your perception will be enhanced tremendously.

Yoni Mudra

It is more advanced than bhramari and should be undertaken after some practise. Sitting in siddhasana close the ears with your thumbs, eyes with index fingers, nostrils with middle fingers and mouth with the two smaller fingers, placing them above and below the two lips. The seven doors should be gently but firmly closed. Inhale deeply and slowly, releasing the middle fingers momentarily. Try to discover the inner sounds emanating from the bindu, middle of the head or the right ear. Hold the breath as long as possible and then release. Now repeat the process as many times as possible. Everytime a new faint sound is heard you should leave the old one and transfer your awareness to the new one. Eventually you are going to discover many sounds, but there is a specific sound which has to be found and concentrated upon. Bindu will be discovered and its benefits will be accrued.

Sahasrar

Sahasrar (crown centre) literally means "one thousand". In fact it is not a chakra since it exists above the head in non physical form, while a chakra is within the realm of psyche and is connected to a plexus or a set of nerves.

Sahasrar represents integration, silence and cosmic consciousness, and is manifested as vibrations and cool breeze. Its positive aspects are - going beyond the duality and above the three states of being or *gunas,* called *tamas* (inertia), *rajas* (activity) and *sattva* (purity). Its negative aspect is disbelief in God.

Sahasrar is the culmination of the journey of kundalini through all the chakras, and the end result of all yoga practices. Its virtues are infinite and can best be represented by a lotus of thousand petals in red or multicolours. It is the infinite void (*shoonya*), the Brahma, both with form (*sakar*) and without form (*nirakar*). No words can describe it since a description will correspond to limitation. When Shakti and Shiva unite, both are annihilated into "One", and the process of self-realisation begins as a series of experiences. The practitioner experiences death (of ego) and this experience has been described by many yogis.

Once identity is lost, the seer, seeing and seen are merged into one "single awareness". I will put the whole set of experiences into three stages: turmoil, death and resurrection. One experiences *samadhi* which has been called by different names, such as, nirvana, enlightenment, self-realisation, cosmic consciousness, etc.

Kundalini tantra is an emotional approach, while *raj yog* of the great sage Patanjali is an intellectual approach to the same end. At the time of writing his famous *yog sutras* around 600 BC when Buddha existed, paranormal powers were seen as highly criticised, since they were obstacles to spiritual progress. This is the reason why Patanjali did not make a mention of kundalini and its powers, and used an entirely different language. He classified samadhi into three categories: *savikalpa* (with fluctuations), *asampragyata* (without awareness) and *nirvikalpa* (without fluctuations). Experiences related to the awakened chakras from mooladhar to ajna correspond to savikalpa samadhi, while those at sahasrar correspond to nirvikalpa. At ajna, savikalpa ends and nirvikalpa begins, leading to enlightenment at sahasrar. Just as one cannot say when childhood ends and youth begins, and when youth ends and old age begins, so, one cannot say when savikalpa ends and asampragyata begins, and when asampragyata ends and nirvikalpa begins. It is fusion of one into another as a continuity. I completely agree with the views of Swami Satyananda Saraswati in regard to this.

Modern Research on Nadis, Chakras and Kundalini

Towards a definition of Nadis

Things in general depend on two poles; for example, light and dark, male and female, negative and positive, Shiva and Shakti, consciousness and energy, conscious and unconscious mind; and in the same pattern one can put tantra and yoga, complementing each other and making the whole. Tantra provides the theoretical philosophy; yoga provides the practical techniques, which supply a validation of the philosophy in terms of personal experiences and eventually lead to higher consciousness. Now to understand the manifestations of cosmic forces one can visualise them as channels, colours, light, sound, etc., at the psychic level. There is an internal connection between the nadis, the body and the mind; there is no separation.

Continuing with the idea of polarity, our mind and body are the results of two modes; such as, right and left brain, conscious and unconscious mind, an anabolic and catabolic metabolism, a parasympathetic and sympathetic nervous system, etc. Even our very existence hangs between life and death. Eventually, realisation came to the yogis that there are three main flows of energy, which were called the three nadis: Ida, Pingla and Sushumna, which manifest body, mind and spirit. In fact, human beings function on two areas—body and mind, that is, Pingla and Ida; the third one, Sushumna— spirit is dormant and it needs to be precipitated through disciplines like yoga, etc.

Nadis are not physical but are defined as *prana*, energy. Ki, Ch'i, etc., for Pingla, and *chitta* or consciousness for Ida. Pingla is the basic energy of life, masculine, positive, yang, active and dynamic. Freud called it the pleasure principle "Eros", and Jung called it conscious, rational, discriminating personality. Ida is the energy within the personality which is feminine, negative, receptive, passive, yin. Freud called it the death instinct, Thanatos and Jung called it anima, the female within — unconscious, intuitive, sentimental and non-discriminating. Pingla is psychosomatic, outwardly directed, providing motivation to the organs for action — the karmendriyas. Ida is somopsychic, inwards directed, controlling sense organs which gives awareness of the physical world — the gyanendriyas.

Two opposing forces in balance create the third more important and hither dormant force, for example, positive and negative electric charges in balance create electro-motive-force which can run the machinery. Similarly, when body or Pingla and mind or Ida are in balance, spiritual energy "sushumna" is precipitated. And this is a major aim of yoga since kundalini awakens successfully through Sushumna only. Ida and Pingla serve the basic needs of the body while Sushumna is the power line leading to cosmic consciousness. The union of opposites leads to "Individuation" of Dr Carl Jung, the third state of spiritual experiences. Most of the time, Ida and Pingla dominate, alternating between 1 to 2 hours, Sushumna comes to dominance for very short periods of few seconds to few minutes only. The aim of yogic discipline is to create a balance between Ida and Pingla and enhance the period of working of Sushumna, which can lead to existence-knowledge-bliss.

A Scientific Analysis

According to Professor Arthur Deikman of the University of Colorado Medical Center, man has two components-biological and psychological, in terms of modern psychology; that is an "action" mode and a "receptive" mode. These correspond to Ida and Pingla in terms of modern psycho-physiology. In his own words (Deikman, 1971, 25:481-91):

"The action mode is a state organised to manipulate the environment. The striated muscle system and the sympathetic nervous system are the dominant physiological agencies. The EEH shows beta waves and baseline muscle tension is increased. The main psychological manifestations of this state are focal attention, object-based logic, heightened boundary perception, and the dominance of formal characteristics over the sensory; shapes and meanings have a preference over colours and textures. The action mode is a state of striving, oriented towards achieving personal goals that range from nutrition, to defense, to obtaining social rewards, plus a variety of symbolic and sensual pleasures, as well as the avoidance of comparable variety of pain."

Thus Ida is the receptive mode, sensory-perceptual system is at work and there is predominance of parasympathetic function. One is static and alpha waves are in formation, there is state of relaxation and haziness, leading to yogic-sleep or yoga-nindra. However, it is not the true state of meditation. True meditative state comes on awakening of Sushumna, when active and passive modes are in balance. One may experience the two modes simultaneously; it is action in inaction and inaction in action, the real spiritual state. As a practical example, you may be driving the car, yet in a state of perfect relaxation. This is inaction in action. In the other situation, you may be sitting in your sofa perfectly relaxed and not doing anything; but internally you may be involved in creative imagination, which may produce spiritual results. This is action in inaction. Under such a situation or in emergencies you may send psychic calls telepathically. The latent faculties are precipitated and brought to surface. This and other happenings are known as "siddhis" or paranormal powers. Nevertheless you are warned not to indulge in siddhis since they make you deviate from the main goal of Self or God Realisation.

Most of us live the active life of Pingla in order to achieve worldly goals. Receptive and passive side of Ida is missing and those are the main reason of us being unhappy. A balance is required, and this is where yoga comes into the picture. A variety of yoga practices precipitate your creative side which can be a productive activity in the subtle field, in addition to bringing peace and inner happiness.

The Nadis and the Brain
Neuroscience on research has shown that the right side of the brain controls the left side of the body, and the left controls the right side. Furthermore, each side of the brain controls the opposite, but complementary mode of consciousness. This scientific finding is in agreement with the views of the yogis. Both science and yoga, working independently and

differently from each other, have arrived at the conclusion that there are two modes of functioning for man. Brain circuits are based on Ida and Pingla, intuition and intellect, consciousness and action.

Left side of the brain is found to be concerned with logic, reasoning, analysis and linear functioning; while right side is intuitive, sentimental, holistic and non linear for knowledge. How intuition works is a mystery for science; but the yogis confidently say that when mind stops, wisdom comes in. Intuition is direct knowledge from beyond, it does not require linear thinking. The right side of the brain corresponds to Ida, and the left to Pingla, as the physical side of nadis. Swami Satyananda Saraswati has given the following list of modes of functions (Saraswati, 1984, 364):

Left Brain (Pingla)	Right Brain (Ida)
analysis	understanding
verbal	spatial
temporal	here and now
partial	holistic
explicit	implicit
argument	experience
intellect	intuition
logic	emotion

thinking	feeling
active	passive
light	dark
conscious	subconscious
talkative	silent
solar	lunar
positive	negative
mathematics	poetry
rational	mystical
law	art
objective	subjective
digital	analogue

It is found that hemisphere governs happiness and positive feelings, and the right brain governs sadness and negative feelings. However, most of us fluctuate from one state to another. Pingla handles likes and Ida handles dislikes. Thus, the things we like are focused and achieved by the left brain; this fits well the active of Pingla nadi. The things we dislike and try to avoid or withdraw from are handled by the right brain which is introvert, receptive and fits well with the mode of Ida nadi.

We generally tend towards external, materialistic and technical Pingla instead of intuitive, subtle and sentimental Ida. However, unless both brains are working together we cannot appreciate the message carried by an allegory or metaphor, or the sentiments of a person or the finger side for that matter. According to Professor Eugene D'Aquili, University of Pennasylvania Medical school, circuits that underlie higher mental states, from flashes of inspiration to altered states of consciousness, lie within the right brain , Ida, and are powered by the emotions (Black, 1982). He formulated a neurological description of "the intuitive perception of God" in which one sees the reality as a whole and experiences a feeling of oneness with the world, According to this research, therefore, right brain is responsible for experiencing consciousness. However, according to the yogis, there should be a balance between the right and the left brain or Ida and Pingla, in order to have experiences of the spiritual order. A meaningful and satisfactory life is lived by only those people who have their right brain equally developed along with the left one. In short, left brain is concerned with materialism while the right is concerned with spirituality. One needs to strike a balance between the two for a worthwhile living.

Importance of balance

It was stated earlier that only when the two opposing things combine in balance, the third more powerful and hidden thing emerges. When the sad and happy hemispheres are balanced for quite some time, a new state emerges that combines logic and intuition, emotions are transformed and a new and more powerful set of neurological activities are possible. Most religions have said so, categorically. The ardhanareeshwara — half Shiva and half Shakti in one body, conveys clearly that when male and female aspects are balanced in a person, he/she becomes Godlike. The same message is conveyed by the hermaphrodite figure of early Christianity, and androgynous figure of Greek mythology. Look at the face of queenAthena of mythical Greece, face of Lord Krishna, face of Lord Jesus Christ — they all carry masculine as well as feminine representations on themselves.

In recent years, Einstein was such an example of equilibrium. In his own words, "The real thing is intuition. A thought comes and I may try to express it in words afterwards." He was a natural yogi who used both sides of his brain. In yogic terms, he must have experienced the awakening of energy or the precipitation of Shakti in his nadis, which must have opened his chakras as well. And for that matter, we can name most of the inventors in various walks of life, from Faraday to Mary Curie, from C. V. Raman to Rabindra Nath Tagore, from Copernicus to Leonardo da Vinci, and so on.

There are situations with exactness, such as, while solving mathematical problems or supervising the production in a factory, etc., where the left brain is required. But there is a time in life when intuition is required. Even in ordinary situations when you are driving your car, you use some intuition about when to shift gears, or when to pass good remarks on others, or what words to use when there is a tense situation. You can see that a balance is required for a worthwhile living. Hatha yoga, Kundalini yoga and Kriya yoga practices have ample exercises and practices to bring about this balance.

Concluding Remarks

It is recommended that practises for each chakra should be done for one month each before passing on to the next. However, one can combine a set of exercises in one, which can be practised daily and a simultaneous awakening of the chakras can be envisaged.

To this end, the following combination is recommended: moolbandh and nasikagra mudra for mooladhar, vajroli/sahajoli mudra for swadhishthan, uddiyan bandh for manipur, ajapa jap for anahat, jalandhar bandh and vipareeta karni asana for vishuddhi, trataka for ajna, and yoni mudra for bindu. Since siddhasana gives best results, and the three bandhs can be combined into one, the list can be made more compact by:-

• Practising pranayama in siddhasana with tribandh (mool, uddiyan, jalandhar, simultaneously) for 20 to 30 minutes.

• Nasikagra mudra, vajroli/sahajoli, vipareeta karni asana, khechari mudra and yoni mudra for 10 to 15 minutes each.

- Ajapa jap for 20 to 30 minutes.
- Trataka for 20 to 30 minutes.
  This is a requirement of two-and-a-half hour everyday, which can awaken all the chakras to the perfection of Kundalini Yoga.

OTHER TITLES IN THE SERIES